YOU'LL SURVIVE!

YOU'LL SURVIVE!

Late Blooming, Early Blooming,
Loneliness, Klutziness, and
Other Problems of Adolescence,
and How to Live Through Them

FRED POWLEDGE

CHARLES SCRIBNER'S SONS · NEW YORK

Copyright © 1986 Fred Powledge

Charles Scribner's Sons
Macmillan Publishing Company
866 Third Avenue, New York, NY 10022
Collier Macmillan Canada, Inc.

Printed in the United States of America

First Edition

3 5 7 9 11 13 15 17 19 F/C 20 18 16 14 12 10 8 6 4 2

Library of Congress Cataloging-in-Publication Data
Powledge, Fred.   You'll survive!
    Includes index.
    Summary: Explores the experience of adolescence, its
physical and emotional stages and the relationships
between teenagers and parents, other adults, peers,
school, the media, and society, and suggests ways of
coping with common problems.
1. Adolescence—Juvenile literature.
2. Puberty—Juvenile literature.
3. Adolescent psychology—Juvenile literature.
[1. Adolescence]   I. Title.
HQ796.P67   1986   305.2′35   85-43351
ISBN 0-684-18632-2

For Marvin Wayne,
who bloomed after all

Contents

1

The Misery and Excitement of Adolescence

If a teen-ager listens in on a gathering of adults who are discussing any of the weightier aspects of human life — happiness, fulfillment, how to raise the kids — the eavesdropper is almost certain to hear at least one reference to a subject that adults think is of great importance: adolescence. And if the teen-ager listens long enough, she or he is bound to hear someone make the point that adolescence — or what the adult can remember of it — is really miserable. The speaker is likely to say that the growing-up years were full of deep, dark fears: the fears that go with being certain you're much too short, or maybe too tall, or too plain-looking, or too flat-chested, or (in the case of a boy) not flat-chested *enough*; fears of bad breath; fears of not being sufficiently popular or athletic; fears of not developing as rapidly or as thoroughly as your peers.

1

You'll Survive!

It all amounts to a miserable, haunting fear of some-how not making it to the other side of adolescence.

And yet our theoretical roomful of complaining people obviously *did* make it to the other side, because they're all here, in their adult clothes and with their adult faces and adult bodies, to tell about it. But it will be clear to our younger listener, snooping at the dining-room door, that adolescence is something that is of exceeding importance to adults. The subject dominates their thoughts and their conversations long after their complexions have cleared and their bodies have assumed their permanent shapes and their pop-ularity and success are more or less established. Adoles-cence, for them, just as for the teen-ager about to go through it, going through it, or just gone through it, is a powerfully important subject.

It's all the more important when the person going through it thinks (correctly or incorrectly, since we often aren't able to appraise ourselves very objectively) that he or she is not developing quickly enough. Our parents may refer to us as "late bloomers," as flowers that open their petals and display their bright colors late in the spring, or perhaps toward the end of the summer. Our parents' tone of voice may be as soothing as a warm bath, but still we wonder. When will I bloom? While I'm waiting to bloom, what am I missing out on? How can I deal with all the humiliation of still

2

looking like a kid when all my classmates are starting to look like grown-ups? And, perhaps worst of all: How can I cope with the unfairness of knowing that I have a very mature brain trapped inside this immature-looking body?

The various stages of adolescence have no clearly defined markings, no easily identified beginnings, middles, and ends, and that adds to the confusion. It's not just late bloomers who worry about late blooming. Because there aren't any precise standards for adolescence, *lots* of young people, including those who would be perfectly average (if we knew what "average" was), are concerned about their development. Perhaps the only kids who aren't worried are the ones who are clearly the early bloomers, the ones whose bodies assume adult shapes very early in the growing-up process. But these young people have plenty of concerns, too, one of them being the knowledge that their emotional development hasn't caught up with their physical growth. So if you suspect you're a late bloomer and you can spare some pity, save it for the gorgeous hunks and beauties among your age group.

Because the phenomenon of late blooming is so widespread — or, rather, the *concern* about late blooming is — it might be termed a national preoccupation among young people. It's not the sort of thing that keeps millions of young men and women awake at night, but it is a preoccupation nonetheless. And, judging from the attention that adults give to the subject at those dinner parties when the matter of adolescence comes up, it's a preoccupation that many of us share long after we've successfully negotiated our way through adolescence.

The author of this book, to name one person whose adolescence is long behind him, was classified firmly in his own mind as a "late bloomer," and childhood consultations with adults in his family confirmed that other people classified him that way, too. I think it's fair to say that I spent a bit of time being miserable over the suspicion (one easily confirmed by looking at a lot of the kids around me) that I looked like a kid long past the time when I thought I should start looking like an adult. But that all changed. I got taller — more than six feet tall, in all — and I became sexually mature (and became the father of someone who's gone through her own bout with adolescence). Sometimes I even act emotionally mature, as well. Some of my baby fat never did seem to leave me, but that's probably explained by my fondness for pizza and Italian bread.

For all these reasons, this book exists. It was conceived as an attempt at helping people get through a period of their lives that is delightful, rewarding, and full of excitement and anticipation, but also scary, confusing, and loaded with apprehension. And, above all, a time of life that is inevitable. Practically everybody makes it through adolescence.

The help in this book comes from several sources. One of them is adults who have made the study of human development their life's work. Some of them are psychologists — as you might suspect, since psychology is the study of the mind and behavior. Others are educators. That's understandable, too, inasmuch as most personal development takes place, in our society at least, during the years when most young people are in school.

Although these scholars have studied adolescence for decades, it can properly be said that they've found the answers to only a few of the questions about why people develop the way they do, when they develop, and what causes that development. The unanswered questions are most abundant when they concern the emotional side of adolescence — the feelings that people have toward themselves and others, and the motivations behind those feelings. But there's considerable lack of agreement on some of the physical aspects of development, too. We still don't know for sure, for example, exactly how our glands perform the tasks of converting the child's body into that of an adult. And we are at our greatest loss for knowledge when it comes to explaining the connections, if and when they exist, between the physical and emotional sides of maturing.

Still, although the scholarly experts admit that they've got an abundance of things to learn about adolescence and adolescents, they've learned a lot, And it is to the benefit of the young person who is interested in the growing-up process to check into this body of knowledge, either to seek help with some personal problem or merely to satisfy a curiosity about what's happening to him.

Other help in this book comes from a completely different group of experts. This is a small but thoughtful number of people who have recently gone through adolescence themselves. These people are old enough so that they are no longer directly involved in the anxieties and glories of adolescence, but they're also young enough so they can clearly recall the experience. Unlike the older people at the dinner party whose memories of adolescence have blurred into a single word, like "miserable" or "fantastic," these young people have the sights and sounds and feelings of adolescence fresh in their minds. The young people who recall their experiences here make up a tiny and unscientifically selected group, however, and the reader shouldn't get the impression that they speak authoritatively for all adolescents everywhere. One of the problems with much of the scientific research that's been done on adolescence is that the people doing the studying sometimes take the experiences of a very few and assume that they are *everybody's* experiences. Nothing could be more unlikely when you're talking about a stage of life that occurs to everyone who reaches adulthood. There are simply too many adolescents, and too many ways of being an adolescent, and too many possible combinations of experiences that can happen in life to allow us to make wildly general statements about the maturing process.

The experts, both those with and those without the formal credentials, offer information that can help you to get safely through the experience of adolescence, to cope with late blooming, and to figure out whom to ask for help. But don't expect them to offer instant cures for adolescence. Adolescence does not lend itself to cure-alls. Besides, adolescence isn't a disease. Adolescence is a situation that everybody goes through. It's one that has its good moments and its bad moments, and the experts who are quoted here are trying to help you deal with, or at the very least understand, the bad ones.

So there aren't any "remedies" or shortcuts through adolescence. What there *is* is the lesson that is extremely simple — so simple that we tend to forget it from time to time. And that's the fact that we're all in this together.

No matter what the problem of adolescence, whether

it's late blooming, early blooming, or even no blooming, parents who don't understand you, or you who don't understand your parents, you're not alone. Young people growing into adults have faced these problems before and survived, and they'll continue to face them and survive.

It's only fairly lately that people have begun to understand the great importance of the fact that, no matter what problems they may be facing, there's always somebody else, and most likely lots of people, who share their same concerns, fears, and anxieties.

The civil rights movement that reached its peak of effectiveness in the American South in the early 1960s probably had a great deal to do with this. It was young, black college students in Greensboro, North Carolina, who took the knowledge shared by millions of black people before them — that society and its institutions of government were not treating them fairly — and turned it into nonviolent direct action of a sort that captured the nation's attention and challenged its conscience — the lunchcounter sit-ins of 1960. The vital middle step, though, lay in spreading the word to individual black people that their grievances were not isolated ones. Once they gathered their strength together, they were able to forever change the face of a nation. They turned what had been thought of as powerlessness into a tremendously powerful movement.

Others were quick to learn the lesson. Groups of

people from other races or ethnic groups found strength and support in the knowledge that there were many others like them who shared their concerns and ambitions. Now it is commonplace to see "support groups" of a great rainbow of people, from gays to physically handicapped to adoptees to computer users.

The adolescent doesn't have to look any farther than the schoolroom, soccer field, or church activity hall to find *his* support group. People who have been through adolescence, or who share some of your same problems of growing up, are all around you. Their advice and help are there for the asking. Of course, you have to be willing to reciprocate with a willing ear and experiences of your own. But that shouldn't be difficult. No matter what adults at dinner parties may say about the miseries of adolescence, the time is a fantastically exciting one. Even the latest bloomer has the joy of watching the bright colors of life deepen as the petals of adulthood unfold.

2

The Voyage

The experts who study adolescents, along with ordinary adults who have gone through the process and a lot of kids who are currently in the midst of it, agree that adolescence is a time of great *confusion*. That word pops up frequently in books about adolescence, in informal discussions about it, and in people's recollections of the years in which they stopped being children.

But "confusion" is just one of the terms that are routinely applied to adolescence and adolescents. There's a whole array of expressions that people have used to try to describe this baffling condition that everybody goes through. Here are some of them:

• Adolescence is "a period of radical change in the total individual," one in which all sorts of changes — physical, emotional, and social — are mixed in together.

• As a form of development, adolescence is unique to human beings. In other primates — apes, monkeys, and similar mammals — changes in glands and the central nervous system take place shortly after birth, and the animal is soon mature. But in humans, the process takes many years.

• Adolescence is a time when people do a lot of things without thinking about them beforehand. This impulsive behavior can be cute, as when a boy's sheer excitement over being alive leads him to dash out of his house and climb a tree to the very top, but it also contributes to mishaps. Accidents are the greatest cause of death in Americans between the ages of fifteen and nineteen; most occur in automobile crashes, drownings, falls, and with firearms.

• Adolescence, says one social scientist, is a kind of island between the two big chunks of human life, childhood and adulthood; between a state of being nurtured and a state of providing nurture.

• An invariable task of someone who is moving through adolescence is the always troubling (but necessary) job of severing the very close ties with her family and then learning how to establish equally close relationships with people who until now have been strangers. Sometimes we describe this as a kind of symbolic cutting of the umbilical cord, the connection that exists between mother and child. These strangers, of course, are the people who will become the loved ones, the husbands and wives and best friends of adulthood.

• Adolescence, says a group of psychiatrists, also is learning "how to work and how to love."

• Lots of people who study adolescence refer to it in terms of a voyage, as if it were a trip on a boat. It's an apt description, for several reasons: Voyages on boats can be unpredictable, with dangers lurking in the form of storms and rocky shores and sometimes (in the sailors' imaginations, at least) a sea monster or two. The sea can be calm or it can be choppy, and most of the time it is a combination of the two. One thing a sailor always wants at the end of the voyage, no matter how much fun the sailing itself may be, is a secure place to tie up to the dock or drop an anchor. All these characteristics of sailing a boat can be applied, without stretching the imagination too much, to going through adolescence (or life in general, for that matter).

The young person, writes one expert, is engaged in a "struggle . . . in finding his adult moorings." And the physical and emotional changes that occur during adolescence, says another, are not "mild ripples" but rather "breakers that flow over the individual and overwhelm him."

Young people have always occupied the thoughts of those who study and comment on human nature. The Greek philosopher Aristotle, who lived from 384 to 322 B.C., devoted some of his famous work, the *Rhetoric*, to an examination of the qualities of the young. (Aristotle referred to them as "young men," but certainly much of his thinking could be applied to young women as well.)

The young, he wrote, were "changeable and fickle in their desires, which are violent while they last, but quickly over: their impulses are keen but not deep-rooted and are like sick people's attacks of hunger and thirst." Youths, he continued, were "hot-tempered and quick-tempered and apt to give way to their anger; bad temper often gets the better of them, for owing to their love of honor they cannot bear being slighted and are indignant if they imagine themselves unfairly treated." (How close this comes to the definition laughingly offered by a modern-day teen-ager: "Adolescence," she said, "is when you think you're treated unfairly. It's when, no matter how you're being treated, basically you think that you ought to be treated differently.")

Aristotle felt that young people tended to "look at the good side rather than the bad, not having yet witnessed many instances of wickedness. They trust others readily, because they have not yet often been cheated. . . . Their lives are mainly spent not in memory but in expectation, for expectation refers to the future, memory to the past, and youth has a long future before it and a short past behind it: on the first day of one's life one has nothing at all to remember, and can only look forward."

Modern-day adolescents and their parents might argue with one of Aristotle's statements. Youths, he said, "are shy, accepting the rules of society in which they have been trained, and not yet believing in any other standard of honor." Because they had not yet been "humbled by life," they believe in high ideals and "exalted notions." Young people "would always rather do noble deeds than useful ones: their lives are regulated more by moral feeling than by reasoning. . . ."

Aristotle continued his list, which turns out to be just as applicable to young people today as it was to those of 2,000 years ago: "They are fonder of their friends, intimates, and companions than older men are, because they like spending their days in the company of others and have not yet come to value either their friends or anything else by their usefulness to themselves. All their mistakes are in the direction of doing things excessively and vehemently."

This tendency toward excess, wrote the philosopher, causes young people to "overdo everything: . . . they love too much and hate too much, and the same with everything else. They think they know everything and are always quite sure about it; this, in fact, is why they overdo everything."

And young people then, as now, liked to have a good time. ". . . They are fond of fun and therefore witty," wrote Aristotle. He defined wit as "well-bred insolence."

It shouldn't be too surprising that many of the comments people make about adolescence and adolescents are expressed in terms of the adolescents' relationships to adults. It's adults, after all, who are making the comments, whether they're psychologists, parents, or Aristotle, and they tend to judge the world by their own standards and rules. What may seem like a perfectly normal event in the life of an adolescent — something like, say, gobbling down four Big Macs in one sitting because you're extremely hungry — is likely to strike an adult as bizarre. Most *adults* don't consume four hamburgers at a sitting, the reasoning goes, so therefore it's unusual when a teen-ager, or anybody else, does it. This may seem like a narrow-minded and selfish way of thinking, but people do it all the time.

Look, for example, at the way we see the rest of the world and universe. We know perfectly well that the Sun is at the center of our own particular solar system, and that Earth and the other planets revolve about it, but we nevertheless continue to speak of the Sun's "setting" and "rising," as if it were *we* who were the center of attraction. And if you're a resident of the United States, chances are the world maps you'll find in your geography books all feature the United States right in the middle of things. But if you're a citizen of, say, Switzerland, "the world" might have Europe in the position of prominence.

So adults tend to view adolescents by adult standards, even though those same adults have gone through the process themselves, sometimes just a few years before, and really ought to be more understanding about the behavior they now see as strange.

All this sounds pretty serious. The picture of the panicking young person, overwhelmed by towering ocean waves that crash over his head, submerged by confusion, getting his head above water only long enough to cut his ties with the people who represent the past, in the meantime thoroughly bewildering all the adults around him — this sounds like a pretty scary deal indeed. Add to this the confusions that could come from thinking you're a late bloomer, and you've got what sounds like a recipe for a lot of trouble.

So why don't we hear more about it? Why hasn't adolescence been declared an epidemic? Why hasn't a National Adolescence Foundation been established to find a cure for it?

The answer is a simple one. Adolescence, as we've said before, happens to everyone — big, small, short, tall, black, brown, late bloomer, early bloomer, just-right bloomer, computer genius, jock, bookworm, boy, girl, farm kid, city kid, you name it. At any given moment in the United States, some 20 percent of our entire population is between the ages of ten and twenty. That's close to 50 million young people, a lot of whom are right in the middle of their "voyages" toward adulthood.

Adolescence, despite the alarming words that sometimes are used to describe it, is not a disorder or a disease. It's *normal.* A life without adolescence is what would be abnormal, because that would mean someone who never made the transition, both painful and delightful as it is, from childhood to adulthood, from a person who only can receive nurture to one who is capable of nurturing. All the bewilderment, confusion, struggle, and pain are important, indispensable elements of becoming an adult. We'd *really* be in trouble if we found a cure for adolescence.

And there's another reason why we needn't get overly worried about adolescence and all its contradictions and confusions: It doesn't last long. It may at times seem like a process that has no end, but in fact it lasts just a few years. Even for kids who think of themselves as late bloomers, the moment is never very far away when the bloom is at its fullest and the serious business starts of being an adult for the rest of your life. Some of the same adults who recall their growing-up years as being "miserable" are likely to refer in almost the same breath to those same years as being "the best years of our lives," a time that is remembered with soft smiles. The fact that some people can remember their adolescence in two separate ways doesn't necessarily mean that they're just fooling themselves. The years of blooming *are* both painful and close to perfect; bewildering and beautiful; full of both guilt and innocence. The important thing to remember is that you'll survive them, just as the rest of the human race has managed to survive them before you.

3

What's Happening to You

Although there's a lot about adolescence that we haven't figured out yet, there's a lot we do know. We can pretty well predict the order in which a person's physical body will change from that of a child to that of an adult, and the social scientists have some fairly good ideas about the psychological changes as well. What is very clear is the fact that, as we've seen before, the speed with which adolescence progresses, and the times when it starts and ends, vary widely.

Sometimes people use the term *puberty* to mean *adolescence*, but there are real differences between the two terms. *Puberty*, which comes from a Latin term meaning "to be covered with hair," begins when activity increases in the glands that control the body's sex hormones.

A gland is a part of the body, often a very tiny one, that takes substances from the body — water and proteins and enzymes — and uses them as raw materials to make chemicals that are important, sometimes absolutely necessary, to life. Glands close to the surface of the skin produce sweat, for example, while those deep inside the bodies of animals churn out chemicals that aid in digestion.

Others, called the endocrine glands, produce hormones that have a lot to do with puberty and adolescence. These chemicals flow through the bloodstream to the organs that need them in order to carry on the organs' specialized or general duties. One of the most important glands from the adolescent's point of view is the pituitary, which is situated beneath the brain and does a lot of work for an organ that's about the size of a pea. It produces hormones that regulate a person's growth, the cycles that govern the function of the sexual life, and other matters. Another is the thyroid gland, situated in the neck, which controls growth. The gonads, in the groin, produce reproductive cells called gametes. In females, this means cells that can turn into the eggs that, if fertilized, can become babies. In males, this means cells that can become the sperm that fertilizes eggs.

Hormones have everything to do with growing up, and with when, how fast, and for how long we grow. Glands regulate the body's growth even before birth, but at puberty they also increase the production of the sex hormones. Science isn't exactly sure how this happens, but it starts with the maturing of certain parts of the body's central nervous system. This system, which is made up of the brain and the spinal cord, is the mass of nerve tissue that controls an animal's life in practically every way.

When this maturing starts, scientists believe, certain chemical and electrical "gates," which through childhood have been closed, are opened, allowing the glands to be stimulated. Now, with the glands at work, the hormones start flowing — the chemicals that produce mature sperm and deeper voices in boys and eggs and breasts in girls, and pubic hair and more active sweat glands in everybody. (Lots of adolescents think, when they start sweating profusely from what seems to be every pore, even the palms of their hands, that their bodies must be rebelling against them violently. Maybe so, but the fact is that so are everybody else's.)

And with the glands clicking away and the hormones trickling through the body's system, the young person becomes a walking advertisement for puberty. There's a sudden and dramatic increase in height and weight (in girls first, because they mature, on average, about two years earlier than boys). Sometimes this results in young people who look as if they have lost control of their feet and legs and arms. They bump into tables, knock over milk cartons, and generally behave in an awkward manner.

This is strange, because tests have shown that adolescents enjoy an increase in their physical strength,

21

their ability to move around, and their coordination during this period. There may be an explanation. The late Irene M. Josselyn, in her book, *The Adolescent and His World,** points out that when an "awkward" adolescent does tasks that are clearly defined — for instance, successfully guiding an inflated ball around other people and through a metal hoop with a net hanging from it, after practicing a good deal — the results may be anything but "awkward." But when the same youth is handed a completely new task to perform, or when he has to respond to a sudden stimulus (like quickly moving his arm across a breakfast table to grab the cornflakes box before his kid sister gets it), he's likely to find himself unfamiliar with his rapidly growing body and to dump the milk on everything, whereupon his parents and kid sister condemn him as "awkward" or a "megaklutz."

The sudden changes in size and weight, which the experts call the "growth spurt," are only the first and most obvious signs that the child is turning into an adult. There are a number of other physical changes in adolescence, and they are listed here. (A reminder: While science is fairly certain about the *sequence* of these changes in both girls and boys, we can't set down any clear rules about *when* the changes take place.)

---

* Irene M. Josselyn, *The Adolescent and His World* (New York: Family Service Association of America, 1952.)

In girls, the sequence usually goes like this: At first, her breasts become larger (inside them, the structures are being built that later will allow her to nurse a baby) and pubic hair appears. (In many cases, though, it's the hair that comes first.) The girl's pelvis broadens, almost certainly because nature is preparing her for the eventual job of delivering a baby, and the baby must emerge through the bowl-shaped bones of the pelvis. Then menstruation begins; a girl's first menstrual period is called *menarche*, a term commonly used by scientists to mark the occurrence of puberty in girls.

Menstruation is an indication of a pregnancy that did not happen. When a woman's egg is fertilized by a man's sperm, it may grow into a child inside an organ called the uterus. The lining of the uterus is actually a layer of nutrients that the woman's body sends there to nourish the baby during its nine months of waiting to be born. When the woman's reproductive system produces an egg (which it usually does every twenty-eight days) that isn't fertilized by sperm from a male, the lining of the uterus disintegrates into menstrual fluid, which looks like blood. The fluid travels from the woman's uterus out the vagina, and the woman "has her period."

After menarche the girl develops axillary hair, which is the dark hair that grows in armpits. And one or more years after the beginning of menstruation, the girl reaches her full reproductive capacity: She is phys-

23

ically and biologically capable of having babies, although she runs a greater risk of having problems with her pregnancy than someone a little older. In our society, she is not generally thought of as *emotionally* ready to become a mother yet, either. She is still a teen-ager, and she has a lot more to learn about life and living, and our culture makes it plain that it wants her to wait a few more years before starting childbearing. Society tries to enforce that desire by setting minimum ages at which people can get married. The age varies from state to state, but for a woman it usually runs around sixteen or seventeen if she has the consent of her parents, and eighteen if she doesn't. (In Alabama, New York, Texas, Utah, and the Virgin Islands a girl as young as fourteen can get married with parents' permission, and in Kansas and New Jersey the age is twelve!)

In boys, the first change after the "growth spurt" is in the testes, which are the sperm-producing, ball-like organs that are enclosed in a sac beneath the penis. The testes grow larger and the sac, which is called the scrotum, becomes redder in color and more wrinkled in texture. Pubic hair appears (in both girls and boys, at first the hair is straight and later it becomes kinky), and then the penis grows larger.

This is a matter of great importance for boys, one that is certainly equal to the concern that girls often express about the size of their breasts. Although science

24

tells us that penis size has practically nothing to do with one's "manhood" and ability to produce the sperm that fertilizes the female egg, lots of boys (and grown men) worry about the size of their sexual organs. Since the size of a penis is less easy to judge in public than the size of a woman's breasts, boys traditionally have tried to satisfy their curiosity by peeking intently at their classmates and friends on those occasions when everybody's together with no clothes on — for instance, in the shower room at school after a physical education class. There's no proof that this really provides insecure adolescent boys with comforting information, but it's a practice that doesn't seem likely to ever end.

The boy's voice starts changing at about this time, and after that he is capable of having his first ejaculation. This happens when the boy becomes sexually excited. Blood flows to the penis and makes it hard, and friction causes a fluid to shoot from the end of the organ. The fluid, which is called semen, contains the sperm that can fertilize eggs, along with other glandular secretions. When a male and a female are having sexual intercourse, or coitus, the friction results from the rubbing of the penis against the walls of the vagina. Ejaculation can occur, also, when the friction is produced by the hand (masturbation) or by unconscious movements (as in ejaculation during sleeping, which is also called nocturnal emission).

You'll Survive!

At about this time, the boy reaches his maximum level of growth. Underarm hair appears, and the boy's voice changes become more apparent. This last happens because the testes have been manufacturing large amounts of the male sex hormone called testosterone. When this chemical reaches the boy's speaking mechanism it makes his larynx larger and his vocal cords longer, and the result is a deeper voice. (Testosterone, which is one of the "male" hormones, has lots of other effects on the body as well, as do estrogens and progesterone, which are thought of as the "female" hormones. To make matters even more complicated, each sex also manufactures small quantities of the other's hormones.)

Finally, the ultimate proof that a boy is becoming a man: facial hair. There is a definite order, researcher J. M. Tanner has written, in which the hairs of the moustache and beard appear on a boy's face. The first ones emerge at the corners of the upper lip; then they spread all over the upper lip; then the upper part of the cheeks; and finally down the sides of the face and across the chin. The total amount of body hair, writes Tanner, seems to depend mostly on heredity.

In both girls and boys, some steps in development are similar. Both get pubic hair, and both get underarm hair. In both, the sweat glands enlarge and sweating becomes noticeable, although it may be more apparent in males. Because the inner structures of some of these close-to-the-surface glands do not enlarge enough to keep up with the increased production of sweat, it's easy for them to get clogged and infected. When that happens the result is something whose name is known and feared by every teen-ager: acne. It's "a common and quite normal affliction characteristic of the adolescent stage," according to a report issued several years ago by an organization called the Committee on Adolescence, which studied the lives of young people for the Group for the Advancement of Psychiatry.

We know that the order in which all this growing up takes place is fairly predictable. If breasts have started to bud, then menarche can't be very far away, and if a boy's voice has started to deepen, he can look forward to a test run with his father's razor. What we *don't* know is *when* all this is going to happen. In a typical group of boys aged thirteen, fourteen, and fifteen, said one expert, the range can run all the way from "practically complete maturity to absolute preadolescence." The same can be said of a typical group of girls aged eleven, twelve, and thirteen. And in all cases, the young people can be said to be developing normally.

The Committee on Adolescence found that the average time range during which boys underwent their genital development — that is, the growth of the testes and penis — was from twelve to sixteen years. But the normal range of years during which such development

27

could occur was much greater: from ten to eighteen years. The growth of breasts occurs in girls on the average at eleven to thirteen and one half years, but the normal range can run from as early as eight years until late in the teens.

"In some adolescents," reported the committee, "these changes occur very slowly and may extend for as long as five or six years. In others the changes may take place much more rapidly and be completed in one or two years."

Science started noticing several years ago that puberty and its stages seemed to be happening earlier to young people throughout the world. Better nutrition, especially in early childhood, and greater freedom from disease were believed to be the reasons for this, and there was even some evidence that people who were exposed to more light matured earlier. Now the tendency toward ever-earlier puberty seems to have halted in the more developed societies.

All this discussion of what happens in puberty, and the great emphasis on the fact that *the order* of what happens is a lot more certain than *when* it happens, should offer some comfort if you think you might be a late bloomer. This is small consolation, of course, to someone whose adult, sophisticated brain and emotions are held hostage inside a child's leftover body and show no signs of ever getting out — of getting a matching grown-up body.

But it happens. It will happen. The scientists and the experts have shown us very clearly that not only is there not a *right* time for physical changes to happen; there's hardly even **a** *normal* time. In a situation like that, it's almost silly to use such terms as "early" and "late bloomer." Furthermore — and this may be hard for the adolescent to believe, but it's true nevertheless — physical development is only half the job of adolescence. You're getting a new you inside your head and heart, too.

4

Beyond the Baby Fat

We know far less about the precise nature of the psychological side of adolescence than we do of the biological, physical side. That shouldn't be too surprising. *Psychology* means the study of the way we think and behave, and people's minds and actions are just too varied to permit us to classify their emotional lives into neat little compartments. Thank goodness for this, we might say; it would be a very boring world if we all felt and acted the same way.

We do know that the biological side of adolescence (*bios* comes from the Greek word meaning "life") and the changes that are produced by the glands and the hormones they secrete have important effects on the psychological side. It is perfectly normal, for example, for all the chemically stimulated growth of the body's sexual organs to lead to a great deal of interest in sex.

30

The changes are exciting, but they also bring a certain amount of apprehension. It's not too hard to see that all this means an end to childhood, with its protection from the rough edges of living, and a beginning of adulthood, with its sometimes overwhelming responsibilities. Adulthood is great (it means, among other things, that you don't have somebody else telling you when to be home on weekend nights) but it also has a lot of obligations (now that you're in charge, what time do *you* think is right to be home on weekend nights?). So there is both excited anticipation and a little fear, and all of this has effects on the emotions and behavior of the adolescent.

It's not surprising that someone who's been waiting all her life to grow up gets a bit frightened when the actual process starts. People feel the same way about their wedding days, and about skiing for the first time down a beautiful, crisply white mountain, and about taking a sailboat out in puffy winds. How the young person deals with all the new and sometimes confusing feelings that come with growing up — how he sorts out what others have taught him about right and wrong, what he has learned from his own experience — is all a vital part of the growing-up system. It is this sorting-out process by which the young person writes her own code of behavior — her own list of what's right and what's wrong and how to act in particular situations. Without this, an adolescent won't become an adult.

As you might suspect, the sequence of events in the psychological growing-up process is less easy to pin down than those in the physical process. A new way of thinking isn't as easily spotted as a few dark hairs on your upper lip.

As your new identity appears, there will come with it a number of conflicts, and you're going to have to deal with those conflicts before you get to those "adult moorings" on the other side of adolescence. Your parents play a big part in all this, just as they've been very important in all the rest of your life.

While you're working out your own set of values, the ones that will carry you into, and perhaps all the way through, adulthood, you're going to be testing everything you've heard before. And a lot of what you've heard and seen all your life can be pretty confusing. Your parents and practically everybody else have always told you, for example, that it's wrong to steal. You might have tried stealing once or twice (many people do; it's just a few who seem to do it all the time), and you may have felt guilty afterwards — maybe so guilty that you returned the item you took.

At the same time you were learning (if you pay even minimal attention to the newspapers and news on radio and television) that not everybody seems to feel as negatively about stealing as you do. The press carries frequent reports of wrongdoing by people in high public office — *big* people, like congressmen and senators and even presidents — and these people, when they're caught, don't seem to have followed the same rules that you and almost certainly they were taught in childhood. Nor do they appear to suffer from the same attacks of guilt. And furthermore, you might notice that they don't get punished very severely, either.

What you've got to do — what childhood has at least partially prepared you to do, and what the experience of adolescence is now urging you to do — is work out your own set of rules about all that. What are your feelings about stealing? About wrongdoing of any sort? What kind of lying, if any, is excusable? If you had an opportunity to take someone else's money, would you do it? Would your answer to that question change if you knew that you wouldn't get caught? If you found someone's billfold on the street, and it contained both a hundred dollars and the name and address of the person who lost it, what would you do?

For lots of young people, issues such as these come up frequently in the place where young people spend so much of their time — school. One example everybody knows about: cheating on tests. It is quite clear that cheating on tests is wrong. Lots of people don't do it, but quite a few people do. Are there *any* circumstances under which you would break this rule? Suppose your school operates on the "honor system," in which you not only are pledged to refrain from cheating yourself but you also promise to turn in anybody else whom you see cheating. If you saw the class bully copying the answers off someone else's test paper, would you turn him in? Suppose the cheater was your best friend?

Questions like this — and a zillion others, including not only matters of social honesty but also those concerning the way you behave sexually, the way you feel about the world of work, and the value you place on education, to mention a few — all have to be dealt with in adolescence. And in the process, you're going to be discarding some of the rules taught you by your parents and grade-school teachers, and modifying others, to make them fit into the identity you're constructing.

This can be pretty rough on your nerves. It means, in a way, that by seeking out your own values you're rejecting your parents, the people who've stood beside you all your life. This can be painful, both for you and for your parents; it can make you feel guilty, and it can make them feel rejected and bewildered and angry. But it is perfectly normal. It happens to all of us. It's part of the process of growing up. Even the feelings of guilt provide you with useful material for practicing, for guilt is an emotion you'll have to cope with (in moderate doses, one hopes) all your life.

A teen-ager living in the midst of all this excitement might well feel the need of an occasional vacation from it. Many young people do take such "rest periods" from the tension. They become deeply involved in hobbies or sports, and this helps take their minds off all the nagging issues of maturity. It's ordinary for the late bloomer, whose less-developed body may make the football team or cheerleading an unlikely possibility, to get wrapped up in a totally separate world — computers, perhaps, or books. Kids who are totally into computers are a fairly recent phenomenon, as are personal and home computers themselves, but bookworms have been around as long as books, and that's a very long time. The author of this book not only was labeled a late bloomer but also had to wear eyeglasses so thick that without them he'd be lost on a football field or probably even in a good-sized swimming pool. So the route to bookworm status was an easy and obvious one to follow. If you lack the cash to become a computer nerd, bookworminess is still an honorable way to spend part of your adolescence.

The important thing to remember here is to not let the *withdrawing* become your main motivation and occupation. Don't become a misanthrope, which is a person who hates and distrusts everybody. It's okay to pull out of society a little bit when you need to, but be sure to leave plenty of room so you can get back in when you're ready.

Boys and girls who are going through the early stages of adolescence may complain loud and long about how the opposite sex is gross and yukky, and at pretty much the same time they may be strongly fascinated by it. In their quest for more experience and information, they may seek out relationships, too — either real ones or ones that exist in their fantasy lives — with adults who are not their parents. School is one place to look for these. When the child was in grade school, she spent most of her time each year with one teacher. Now, in junior high and high school, there are many teachers, and that means many opportunities to investigate the philosophies and life styles of different people. The adolescent who is gathering his own set of values and standards wants to sample those of others, picking and choosing and rejecting what doesn't seem right to him.

The relationships don't have to be with people you see every day, or even people you see at all. Young people (and a lot of older ones, too) become interested in the lives of celebrities — football players, pop singers, poets, actors — and study *their* lives, too, for ingredients to add to the recipe.

It's an exciting prospect, when you think about it: You're creating the person you're going to be for the rest of your life. You're taking a thought here, a look there, a frame of mind from here, a way of walking from there, and putting it all into your identity-generator and producing an adult who is different from all other people on earth. Unfortunately, the adolescent is probably so busy coping with the changes of his life that he can't appreciate this fact sufficiently.

It's at times like this that the peer group — the group of people your own age whom you run with — becomes very important to the adolescent's life. The peer group has its own way of talking, its own culture, and — most of all — its own set of rules. It is very helpful in guiding its members toward socially acceptable behavior. Using a kind of informal way of putting together facts and opinions, it figures out ways to solve problems that the young person probably couldn't handle on her own. And the peer group is a very handy way for the adolescent to keep reminded of a very important fact: You're not alone in all this. There are a lot of other people going through it with you.

One of the services that the peer group provides for its young members is a constant reminder that they should conform to the group's rules. Although we think of these as rules, they are laws that are never written down and possibly never even discussed formally. But

they are laws nonetheless, with all the force and
authority of laws passed by Congress. The teen-ager
knows from his or her group, without ever asking,
whether a particular musical group is in or out,
whether it's all right to wear a certain hairstyle or piece
of clothing. Peer groups have always provided these
services. For a few years in the great, distant past, for
example, in Raleigh, North Carolina, where the author
grew up, it was unforgivable for boys to wear their blue
jeans in any way but with one leg rolled up higher than
the other. At the same time it was considered "cool"
for a boy to wear chartreuse pants and to have a key
chain that stretched from the belt almost to the ground
and back.

So the peer group sends the message to conform, and
it's one that is welcomed by the young person. But it's
also rejected. For at the same time the teen-ager is
welcoming the security of the group, she is creating her
independent self. She is becoming unique. This is just
one of the ways in which you're pulled by opposing
forces, just one of the reasons adults might think of
you as bewildered and bewildering, and certainly confused and confusing.

The rest of society, the part of it that's dominated by
adults, wants you to conform, too. The people around
you who run things — parents, teachers, police officers,
school crossing guards, the people you play trick or
treat on every October thirty-first — have until now

tolerated a certain amount of your foolishness. You were, after all, "only a child," and someone who's "only a child" is *expected* to throw a tantrum every now and then, to burst into tears unexpectedly, to push around his younger brothers or sisters for no clear reason, to complain of persecution when someone asks her to keep her promise to walk the dog.

Adult society will still let you get away with acting silly and irresponsible, even though you're no longer "only a child." Being "only a teen-ager" is almost as good an excuse. But the adults are starting to send another message, too: Start acting like a grown-up. Get serious. Conform to *our* rules. Shape up or ship out. The ways in which the teen-ager responds to these demands all become part of the identity he's building for himself.

As you leave the beginning of puberty and make your way into the high-school years, society will have more and more opportunities to deliver these messages to you. In grade school, as we noted before, it's likely that most of your contact with the adult world was with one teacher, and that teacher's relationship with you was very close to that of parent. Now, however, you find yourself with lots of teachers — one for mathematics, one for a foreign language, one for English, another for physical education — and your contacts with the adult world grow.

You might find a job in a fast-food place or at a

supermarket checkout counter, and if you do you'll come in daily touch with the grown-up worlds of finance, responsibility, and relationships with other people, some of whom will be total strangers.

Society, in the meantime, will begin to allow you certain rights that you didn't enjoy before. When you are at the age of sixteen or eighteen, most states will let you apply for a driver's license and drive a car. (It's fifteen in Hawaii and Mississippi.) The national government will allow you — may *order* you — to enter the military, if you're male, at the age of eighteen. On that same magic birthday you can vote in national elections. States vary in their rules about the minimum age for purchasing liquor, with most between nineteen and twenty-one.

The great lack of uniformity in all these ages demonstrates just how uncertain society is about how to define the age at which someone becomes an "adult." This was shown also a few years ago when the voting age was reduced to eighteen from twenty-one — quite a jump, when you think about it. Twenty-one is the last major hurdle toward adulthood for most people. When you hit that ancient figure, you have pretty full rights as an American citizen. You can't become president until you're thirty-five, however, and you can't get a senior citizen's reduced-price ticket for bus rides and ball games until much later.

While adult society is waiting for you to meet its

own somewhat confused requirements for adulthood, it's making increasing demands on you to "act grown-up" — to stop the foolishness of childhood and get down to the business of being mature. But because that same society refuses to let you have all the rights of adulthood (to stay up as late as you want and drive a car when you think you're old enough, for example), you find yourself in a situation that's like the one that infuriated a lot of Americans before the Revolutionary War, the ones whose slogan was, "Taxation without representation is tyranny." How can you act like an adult if they insist on letting you have only a child's rights?

Actually, the late bloomer may find herself at a slight advantage over the early bloomer here. If a fourteen-year-old developed early and *looks* like an adult, with the adult insignia of broad shoulders or curvy chest, the adult world is likely to expect him or her to behave like a grown-up. But if another fourteen-year-old is still waiting to fully blossom, adults may not hold him to the same high standard. He might be able to get away with "childish" behavior for a little longer. Some people might view that as an advantage, some as a disadvantage. In any case, it won't last long. Soon, the late bloomer will bloom, just as the early bloomer did.

One of the most profound changes of the psychological side of adolescence, and one that runs through all the others, is the young person's discovery of himself

41

as a sexual creature. In the early days of adolescence, the changes in the glands were a cause for wonderment and apprehension. Now the maturing adolescent sees sex as something to explore. Some kids examine it with each other by talking about it, while some go further than that. Some explore their bodies by themselves. What you've been taught in your life so far plays an important role in how you handle this stage of your life, as do the rules and standards you've been developing for yourself about what is right and what is wrong and what is in between.

No matter how your exploration takes place, all adolescents are subject to the sometimes confusing fact that has faced young people in our culture for centuries: At the very time when people are biologically ready to make love and have babies, adult society is at its busiest, telling them that they shouldn't. This has been the case for a long time, and it's likely it will stay the case for a long time to come.

A lot of the growing-up process is seen by adults and by adolescents as a matter of sex — sex glands, sex organs, sexual fantasies and thoughts — but that's not all there is to blooming. The young person is a factory producing all kinds of things other than testosterone and progesterone; she and he are turning out bushels of emotions, the chief of which are concern and love for the world around them. The Committee on Adolescence put it this way: ". . . the urge to love expresses itself in many ways. Some of the love feelings are directed to the self, some to people, and some to other objects such as pets, automobiles, books, and scientific projects; and, finally, some of these feelings can seize onto ideas or causes — which then become ideals."

Ideals, after all, are what keep the society going. Children grow up, see the world a bit differently from their parents, see injustices that need correcting and rules that need changing, and as they become young adults they apply their idealism to the world they have inherited. To be sure, some people make it through adolescence with a lot less or more idealism than others. Some people are willing to die for a cause in which they believe, while others couldn't care less. But adolescence serves as a great place for ideals and conviction to grow. Without adolescence, and without the steady quantities of adults it produces, the world would be a boring old place indeed.

5

Society and the Adolescent

The adult world may fall short in offering help to people going through adolescence. And, by telling the young person, "You've got to become an adult like us" but failing to provide an easy-to-read map showing how to do it, society may actually hinder the voyage.

That's not the way adolescence has been treated in lots of other cultures during Earth's history, however. Anthropologists (those who study human beings) and others who have looked at the world's various and diverse societies, both modern ones and those of the past, sometimes speak of "primitive" cultures and the rituals and philosophies they use. When we use the word "primitive" in everyday language we sometimes mean "crude," but technically (back again to the Latin) it is related to the word "prime," which means "first." What the anthropologists usually mean, then, when they talk about a primitive culture is one that evolved early in our history, or perhaps one that has been around a long time and, for one reason or another, has resisted change. It hasn't become "modern."

Sometimes isolation is a reason why a culture has remained primitive. For example, there are parts of New Guinea, in the South Pacific, where people get along very nicely without many of the things we have come to take for granted — television sets, cars, and all the fuel bills we must pay in order to run them. They went without practically any contact with the later-developing societies until forty years ago, when World War II brought airplanes, huge ships, and many strange-acting foreigners into their lives.

Primitive cultures, it turns out, may have done a better job of helping their young people through adolescence than we're doing with what we think of as our modern, sophisticated ways.

In some of them, a clear line has been established, by tradition and experience, between childhood and adulthood. Young people needn't worry about which side they're on: There's a ceremony marking the occasion, and it's unmistakable. The young person is the star of the ritual.

These events, called *rites of passage,* refer to the rituals that a group uses to mark the movement of its individual members through the several important stages of life. These include birth, marriage, illness, death, and — especially — puberty. In some cases, the timing of the ceremony is tied to physical development in young people — the arrival of menstruation in a girl is a logical milestone — while in others it takes place after the boy or girl has completed certain tests. And sometimes the rite is held for a group of young people, all of whom are approximately the same age.

These ceremonies, then, might eliminate some of the confusion and apprehension that can infect young people who think of themselves as late bloomers. After the ceremony, you have the same status as everybody else who passed through it with you, no matter how tall or short or muscular you may be. The famous anthropologist Ruth Benedict pointed out more than fifty years ago in her book, *Patterns of Culture,** that these rites of passage were not so concerned with the biological aspects of adolescence — the physical and glandular changes — as they were the social aspects. "The puberty they recognize is social," wrote Benedict, "and the ceremonies are a recognition in some fashion or other of the child's new status of adulthood."

Such ceremonies might seem to be an all-round good deal for the cultures that have them and the young people who go through them. Another expert in the field, the psychiatrist Irene M. Josselyn, wrote in *The Adolescent and His World*: "In our culture, society not only makes heavy demands upon the adolescent, but it fails to provide him with a preconceived and care-

---

* Ruth Benedict, *Patterns of Culture* (New York: Mentor, 1934).

fully outlined pattern to help him meet these demands. This is in contrast to many of the primitive cultures. The initiation ceremonies in primitive cultures establish an arbitrary line between childhood and adulthood. Prohibitions and sanctions govern, define, and free the behavior of childhood. At a certain point, with ritualistic ceremony, the individual is made an adult. From that time on he is expected to live in the adult world according to a defined code."

Josselyn further writes that customs and taboos are clearly laid out for the new adult, and they "give him a framework in which to develop his own personality." An American adolescent might whine and plead and argue with her parents about how late she can stay out on school nights, but in the primitive societies such rules are not subject to argument. "It is not for the young adult to decide whether or not he will obey them," writes Josselyn; "failure to do so results in arbitrary punishment while compliance results in acceptance."

Menstruation is a convenient, easy-to-determine way to choose the girls who are to go through the rites of passage, but with boys it's a little more difficult. For that reason, some primitive societies have come up with a home-made way of identifying the boys who have participated in the process. It is circumcision, or the removal of the skin at the tip of the penis. Jews and many others perform the quick, simple operation shortly after the boy is born, but it occurs at adolescence in some of the primitive (and even modern) cultures of the world. Some of the circumcision ceremonies are very painful for the boy — a reminder that the voyage from childhood to adulthood is an important one — but in all cases they leave him with physical evidence of his new status. Some cultures use other means of marking or scarring their adolescents, such as piercing holes through their noses and pulling out their fingernails.

Anthropologists have noticed that the rituals often are connected very closely to what the society thinks is important in life. If a group of people is devoted to warfare, for example, then it is going to place great emphasis on training its young men to become warriors. But in other societies, where the emphasis might be on skill at hunting, the ritual might require boys to pass several tests with the bow and arrow.

Among native peoples in British Columbia, Canada, for example, boys rolled stones down hillsides and raced them to the bottom, to show they were swift for hunting game. Girls dropped stones down inside their dresses so that their babies would be born as easily as the stone fell to the ground.

Among a few cultures, not much fuss at all was made over boys, while adolescent girls were the center of attention. In one of them, a girl who had just started menstruating was considered to have great power, and people came to seek her blessing and to ask her to put an end to their illnesses.

Some rites of passage, like some of the circumcision ceremonies, were clearly ordeals for the young people who went through them (and *everybody* went through them, or else they were denied a permanent place in the life of the group). Some male children of the Zuni Indians of the American Southwest were whipped, not because they had been bad but rather to get rid of the bad spirits that dwelled in them. At the end of the ceremony, however, the adults who had been doing the whipping placed their ceremonial masks on the boys and handed them the whips, and the youths whipped the whippers. In other societies, a big part of the puberty ritual was the vision quest, in which a young person (usually male) went off to a sacred lake or mountain and remained, cold and hungry, until he felt he had made personal contact with a supernatural force that would be his helper through life.

All these rituals were important for the life of the community, because in formally bringing children into adulthood they were also bringing new people into the work force — whether the "work force" consisted of a group of warriors, a population of women who could weave, cook, farm, or have babies, or the group that went hunting for game. Because of this, adults made sure that adolescents had plenty of incentive to make the change into adulthood. Among some American

Indians and natives of the Arctic regions, adults refused to let young people eat the most desirable foods — young seal meat, eggs, entrails, heart, liver, small game, or narwhal (a form of whale) — until they had demonstrated that they were skilled hunters. In other cultures, boys who hadn't yet been through the ceremonies were given only cold food to eat. All these restrictions made a child think twice about hanging around in childhood any longer than necessary.

Few of these rituals exist nowadays, but one that does, the bar mitzvah of the Jewish culture, is an important one. The term means "son of the law" in Hebrew, and the law in question refers to the laws and customs of the Jewish religion. The ceremony usually is held in a synagogue or temple on the Saturday closest to a boy's thirteenth birthday, and sometimes it's the occasion for a feast, with dancing, eating, and music. One of the most important of the gifts the boy may receive comes from his father. It is a tallis, or shawl to be worn when praying.

The bar mitzvah serves as a symbol for the time in a boy's life when he is supposed to begin thinking and acting like an adult. One of his responsibilities is to observe 613 holy commandments. More recently, Jewish girls have been having their own coming-of-age ceremonies, called bas mitzvah, when they reach the age of twelve. And among some Americans in general "sweet sixteen" parties are often used to mark a young woman's passage through adolescence.

Generally speaking, then, American society doesn't do a particularly bang-up job of providing a clear-cut certificate for its young people when they become adults. We take great care with *other* rites of passage — baptism, graduation, marriage, funerals, even parties for our older coworkers when they retire — but we stumble around when it comes to puberty and adolescence.

There's another way in which society makes life harder on the adolescent than it needs to be, and that's the way it portrays people in the media. Particularly on television (but also in radio, newspapers, magazines, books, and movies), people often are shown as a lot more shallow-minded, violent, money-grubbing, sex-crazed, and pretty than they are in real life. The result is even more confusion for the adolescent, who is forming an impression of society and deciding on the makeup of his own adult personality. Police officers on television are frequently shown to be brutal and eager to break the law themselves, although they never get punished for it. Many parents are divorced. Most everybody is white. People hardly ever wear seat belts when they drive cars. Adults seem to be always having an alcoholic drink. All that distortion of life goes for people in general. It's even worse when the media turn their attention to young people.

Young people on television are almost always full of wisecracks (usually directed at the somewhat bumbling adult members of their world), very sexually mature, and interested only in having a good time. They hardly ever show concern about school, have relationships with other people that aren't primarily sexual, or engage in serious dealings with adults. Acne doesn't exist on television — except in commercials. There aren't even many people on the tube who wear glasses, although half of the nation's real population does.

A group called the National Commission of Working Women studied for one television season all the prime-time network programs that featured characters younger than eighteen. The study, published in the middle of 1985, was critical of the way television shows children and their relationships with adults. The TV children, said the report, were more likely than real-life children to be wealthy, white, and the offspring of divorced parents. On those rare occasions when shows dealt with serious problems such as racial discrimination, the difficulties were all solved by the end of the program.

Sue Ashton, a young woman who recently went through adolescence herself, says television also ignores a large segment of the teen-aged population. "There are very few shows," she said in an interview, "that have any girl who's between the ages of nine and seventeen. Everybody's either a little girl or a curvy young woman. You have to be either a tiny girl or one of the curvaceous blondes on a detective show. The few teen-aged girls who are in situation comedies now do *not* have flat chests or wear thick glasses or act as if they're insecure. They're all high-school cheerleaders." Sue's solution to this problem was the same that she used to deal with the rest of television's deficiencies: She just didn't take television seriously.

Unfortunately, there are other parts of the young person's life that cannot be ignored as easily as empty-headed situation comedies on television. Whether the adult world knows it or admits it, drugs are a part of the lives of very many young people — either because they have taken drugs or are taking them, or because there is so much discussion of the topic around them by their friends. The adolescent who is not exposed to what has been called the "drug culture" is a rare one indeed.

To a degree that is horrifying to many adults — even those who take illegal drugs themselves, for what they may call "recreational" purposes — young people are experimenting with easily available, but illegal, drugs.

(And they have been experimenting with the legal ones, such as alcohol and nicotine, for a much longer time.)

These drugs produce a great variety of reactions in the young people who use them. Some become very dependent, others experiment a little and then decide to leave drugs behind. Some people are damaged physically or mentally by these substances — and in some cases, the experts believe, are pushed into suicide by them.

As with everything else that goes on during the change from childhood to adolescence, the ways in which a young person feels about drugs is determined by a lot of things that have happened before in that person's life: What he or she was taught as a child to be right and wrong; the examples that are set by those around the teen-ager, both by parents and other adults and by one's peers; and what finally comes out of the adolescent's own personal machinery for building rules and standards and values. The fact that many adolescents, even those who have experimented heavily with drugs, turn away from them and make productive lives for themselves is proof that young people are capable of making sensible, adult decisions.

Many adults can't understand why their children would fall into the trap of depending on drugs in the first place. Nobody knows the real answer, but one suggestion comes from Tina deVaron, a Boston student who contributed an essay to a scholarly book on the subject of early adolescence.* All the other articles in the book were written by experts in the field of human development — anthropologists, psychologists, educators. Tina deVaron, who was 17 at the time the book was published, offered the only report from the adolescent battlefield itself.

The adolescent's life, she wrote, is full of conflicts of all sorts. In response to those stresses, she said, the young person has to construct "a device which keeps him from being hurt and from hurting himself. . . . The easiest thing for him to do is to build a wall."

The wall, she said, can be built out of sarcasm — pretending not to take anything too seriously, mocking at everything that happens in one's life. Or the young person can start acting like someone who is "hopelessly messed up." This, wrote Tina, makes other people pay attention to the adolescent (that helps in his fight against loneliness) "and protects him from having to come out of himself or forget about himself."

The problem with the wall, though, is that the young person must constantly work to keep it up. She can't relax when the wall of isolation is up. And that leads to

---

* Jerome Kagan and Robert Coles, eds. *12 to 16: Early Adolescence* (New York: Norton, 1972).

loneliness. "Loneliness plays a large part in adolescence," writes Tina. And that is when drugs can enter the picture.

Drugs can make the adolescent feel less tense and give him the impression (a wrong one) that he has no problems. And acting as if you're stoned all the time (or actually being stoned) can be used as an excuse for doing the wrong thing. "Drugs can be abused," wrote Tina, "if nothing else eases the tension. The adolescent can find himself depending on dope for all his relaxation. Nobody wants to be in that position."

The rest of the world, then, can be a complicating factor in adolescence. By making demands on the young person and then refusing to tell her how to meet those demands, it can make the journey much more difficult than it needs to be. By filling its media with comic, incorrect examples of what people are really like and how they handle such serious issues as personal emotions, social problems, religion, justice, and discrimination, the adult world is further confusing the young person about what life is really all about. By offering drugs to the teen-ager and then expressing its horrified amazement when he takes them, the adult world is not only sending confusing signals but also showing that it's hypocritical.

But it's always been that way. Even when there was no television, the grown-up world managed to misinform its youth about right and wrong. Even before marijuana and cocaine became so easily available, young people were getting contrary signals from adults about the wisdom of drinking whiskey and smoking cigarettes. The adolescent has always been able to sift through the large number of conflicting rules, regulations, standards, values, and assorted bits of wisdom to come up with his and her own sets of rules. It's the way a new adult generation gets created.

6

Early, Medium, and Late Blooming

If going through puberty and adolescence is sometimes tough — if it's not all peaches and cream watching yourself get "awkward," questioning the things your parents have taught you all your life, coping with big, important issues like drugs and sex — then doing this as a late bloomer must be even tougher.

For some people, it is tough indeed. But the following statement, one of the most overworked ones there is, happens to be true in the case of adolescence: If you just hang in there, it'll all turn out okay. You'll make it to the other side. Educators, psychologists, and others who have studied human development are pretty much in agreement that late bloomers, early bloomers, and just-right bloomers all catch up with one another in the end.

These experts seem so sure of this fact that they spend little of their time studying late blooming and the problems it causes. Instead, they concentrate on the *sequence* of events in puberty and adolescence (the events discussed in Chapter 3). They have found that it's still true, as it always has been, that girls reach puberty about two years earlier than boys, and that the range of development is so great that some boys and some girls will have finished their development before others the same age have started theirs.

The experts also have recorded some social differences between young people who develop early and those who develop later. J. M. Tanner, of the Institute of Child Health at the University of London, has written that boys whose development is more advanced are more likely to be ahead of their peers in athletic achievement and sexual interests. The late developer, wrote the researcher, "is the one who all too often loses out in the rough and tumble of the adolescent world; and he may begin to wonder whether he will ever develop his body properly or be as well endowed sexually as those others he has seen developing around him."

Tanner has more disturbing news for late bloomers, too. Early bloomers, he has written, may turn out later in their lives to be "more stable, more sociable, less neurotic, and more successful in society, at least in the United States." (Someone who is neurotic is afflicted with an emotional disorder, but not necessarily one that keeps that person from living a productive life. A person who complains all the time about being unhappy, or who stuffs himself with candy bars night and day, might be classified as neurotic.)

Tanner also has a tidbit of good news for late bloomers. Girls and boys who look physically mature early in their lives are sometimes embarrassed by that fact, he writes, and they are bothered and confused by adult society's demands that they *act* like the grownups they appear to be.

Regardless of what the experts do and do not know about late blooming, a little serious thinking about the matter should lead you to the conclusion that early physical development is not the most important thing in the world, that the identity you're creating inside your mind and heart is far more important than how many curves your body has and where it has them, and that — to say it again — it all evens out in the end.

Look around at the adults in your world: Your parents, your teachers, television talk show hosts, the people who deliver the mail and ring up sales in the supermarket, the strangers you see on the street. Can you tell from looking at them now which ones were, and which ones weren't, late bloomers? Maybe it's not the biggest deal in the world after all.

The *real* experts, of course, are the young people who have recently been through adolescence. They're no longer caught up in the agonies and joys of the process, but neither have they been away from adolescence so long that they, like many older adults, have forgotten what it was like. Any young person starting through adolescence might do well to interview a sixteen- or eighteen-year-old on what the voyage is all about and how to make it.

For Rebecca Wolff, adolescence started off with what she thought of as a cruel joke. It gave breasts to her closest friends long before she got hers. It didn't help that her two closest friends were a little older than she. "I was dying to get breasts and my period and everything like that," recalled Rebecca, who is now seventeen. "I wanted to be like my friends."

Her mother was as helpful as she could be, said Rebecca, reminding her that her friends were older. If anybody had said the usual cliché — "Don't worry; you've got your whole life ahead of you" — it wouldn't have provided Rebecca with any comfort. "You don't think in terms of having your whole life ahead of you," she said. "Because right then, when you're going through it, it's the *most immediate thing* in your life. When it happened to me, I was eleven. And when I was eleven, I couldn't think in terms of having my whole life ahead of me. I thought I was already grown-up. I thought that I had finished maturing, basically, and I'd just stay the same, only I would get taller.

"You don't think in terms of catching up with the

other kids at all. You can't think beyond the year you're in. Maybe you can, but it doesn't help." Nor does it help a lot to know and be told that the great majority of all the evidence we have — scientific, medical, just the evidence that our eyes bring us — is that pretty soon a late bloomer's body will change. "It's comforting," said Rebecca. "You say, 'I know, I know.' But you also say, 'But what am I going to do *now?* What am I going to do about the fact that in this T-shirt I look ridiculous?' "

Rebecca's problems (and those of many others who find themselves in her situation) were magnified by the feeling she had that in her brain, she was already mature. "Intellectually I always considered myself an adult," she said. "I guess everybody does. I thought I was *more* mature than my friends." The problem, she said, was that at that age girls are very interested in being thought of as attractive by boys. She knew that intellectually she would have just as much as anybody else to put into a boy-girl relationship, "but nobody will look at me because I don't have big breasts."

Rebecca also felt bad because she didn't look like Brooke Shields. At about the time Rebecca hit puberty, Shields became one of the first teen-aged models to get a lot of national publicity. She was everywhere, on magazine covers and in advertisements, seeming to act much more mature and sexy than her age. "Brooke

Shields really changed my life," recalled Rebecca, "because I *wanted to be* Brooke Shields."

Now Rebecca has a fine figure to match her quick wit and mature brain, and she can afford to look back on some of the feelings she had just a few short years ago and smile at them. She recalls, too, the things that helped her most to get through adolescence with a minimum of damage.

One of them was being a bookworm and "brain." It was a role that Rebecca was prepared for, because she was interested in books and smart anyway, but she feels that her physical situation pushed her in that direction, too.

"Among the three of us — me and my two best friends — it was my friends who were really pretty," she remembered. "And I had glasses and stringy hair and I was fat. So what *I* did was be, like, 'the intelligent one.' I tried to act mature. I really got into books. My bookworm stage lasted from about second grade until the end of high school, basically." Rebecca's friends, and even classmates who didn't know her well, seemed to respect her for this intense interest in books — she even got to be known as an accomplished poet — and nobody condemned her for it. All this helped (although at the time Rebecca didn't think of it this way) to set Rebecca apart from the others. It helped her start establishing her unique identity. Rebecca felt that some of her classmates, and both of her best friends, already *had* some of their identity established for them, by being so attractive and mature-looking. So she went out and built her own.

The other thing that sustained Rebecca during her years of waiting for her body to catch up with her mind was friendship. When she had a problem, a worry, a fear, a question, she often went to her parents, but there comes a time during adolescence (and it comes frequently) when parents are just not the best people to talk to. That's when one's friends come in. "These are the people you can go to and say 'Oh, my God, my thighs are so fat!' " explained Rebecca. These are the people who, in everybody's life, are known as "best friends." Rebecca said she's had maybe seven or eight best friends in her life so far. They come in groups of two or three.

These people serve all the usual purposes of friends, but in Rebecca's case they offered a bonus. Because most of them were older than Rebecca, both in years and in physical development, she was able to question them about their experience in the widening world of growing up. She never thought about dumping these girls and seeking out new friends who also had glasses, stringy hair, flat chests, and fat thighs. "You don't get rid of your friends so easily," she said. "And also, that's part of the attraction of those older friends: they're something that you want to be. And they have a lot of information. As much as my mom told me about sex, *she's* not going to give me all the gory details."

Rebecca never did stop being a bookworm. Like many people, she didn't really learn to appreciate the experience of adolescence until she became an adult. "As soon as I knew what adolescence was," she said not long ago, "I thought I was over with it."

Sue Ashton, the eighteen-year-old who commented in the last chapter on the ways in which the media ignore adolescents and their real problems, never feared that she was a late bloomer herself, but she clearly remembers some of the painful moments of growing into adulthood. Like many people, when she remembers an event, she's not likely to recall it in terms of how old she was at the time, but rather what grade she was in at school. This demonstrates just how important school is in lives of adolescents.

"My worst years," says Sue, "were not ninth, tenth, eleventh, and twelfth grades. They were without doubt the sixth, seventh, and eighth grades. I've talked this over with a lot of girls, and they agree. Seventh and eighth grades are just absolutely horrible, because that's the point at which the differences between boys and girls are just so extreme, both emotionally and physically. High school may be pretty harsh, but seventh and eighth grades take the cake."

A girl in those grades, she explained, is likely to be

quite physically advanced over boys her age and may feel ready to begin living an entirely new sort of social life. "You *feel* that you ought to be doing all the high school things," said Sue. "All the things the media tell you that you ought to want to do: the dating, the football games, and all that. And these things aren't even within the realm of possibility for seventh and eighth graders because they're dealing with boys who are just so much younger."

Someone who's going through the process, Sue said, learns quickly that adolescence has two distinct sides, the physical and the emotional. She agreed with Rebecca Wolff that adolescents are likely to think they're a lot more grown-up than their bodies show and that about the time you start figuring out what's happening to you, adolescence is all over. "You *think* it's something that's going to be going on forever," said Sue. "You think that everybody's always going to be ahead of you. This feeling's probably the most intense, for girls at least, at about the age of fourteen. It's a pretty big preoccupation then. Consciously, you know that it'll be over, but your heart tells you it's going to take forever. And then after that it doesn't seem to matter so much anymore."

The difficulties of adolescence, said Sue, can be reduced a lot if you have the good luck to be born into a family with lots of brothers and sisters. Sue, who is the second oldest of five sisters, put it this way: "I think the kids who are more worried about whether they are late bloomers or not are generally not kids from large families. When you're from a large family, you've got kids around you who are either younger or older than you. You can compare yourself with them. You can't do that when you're an only child, or maybe just a younger child.

"In a large family, you constantly have somebody around you who is probably going to be a lot more immature, or a lot more mature. You have an automatic, built-in explanation for the things that happen when somebody's growing up, like how your body grows, and getting your period, and things like that. You've got proof that where you are is okay and natural because this person you're looking at has been right there before you. You remember what she was like when she was your age."

Sometimes, she added, the comparison can work against you. "Your parents can tell you, when you're, say, thirteen, 'Oh, when your older sisters or brothers were thirteen *they* were so much more cool and grown-up and mature and all that.' And you look at yourself and see that *you're* such a mess at thirteen. But at least you know that there's a change that will be coming. You've got the comparisons laid out for you."

It helps, too, she said, to have proof in your own house that older does not necessarily mean more mature. "You see your older siblings at their worst, too," she said. "You might know that one of them actually had a hysterical fit last week because of some tiny thing. Nobody in *school* knows about that, but you know she was weeping horribly for an hour before the big dance. Or that she had to stuff her bra. There're a lot of juicy tidbits that you know about your siblings' insecurities that will make you feel a little bit better about your own. "When you're an only child, you think that your insecurities grow only out of your own problems, when the truth is that they're a lot more natural than you know. Everybody has them."

Many kids aren't fortunate enough to have large families, though. What does Sue recommend for them?

"One's peers," she replied, without hesitating. "Kids you know at school. There's got to be *somebody* you can talk to and compare notes with. You can't even get away with saying 'I'm the shortest person in my class'; no matter what the issue is, there's going to be somebody else somewhere who's got a similar problem."

Why couldn't somebody who felt he was a late bloomer just drop back a few years in terms of his peers — start hanging around with people who are a couple of years younger than he, but who are at the same level of physical development? "I think there'd be too much social pressure to not do that," said Sue. "It's better to be a late bloomer when you're thirteen or fourteen than to have to hang out with ten- and eleven-year-olds. Because that's *admitting* your problem. It's different, of course, if you were in that younger group all along. Maybe you started school a year late so you've always been with that group. But never would you drop back. That's a lot more than just admitting defeat; it's just not done at all."

Sue said she realized how shallow were the words of "encouragement" that sometimes are offered adolescents who are concerned about all the problems that face young people during those years. "Saying 'You'll grow out of it' doesn't help much," she said, "although it's true. What you can do is try to develop a *philosophy* about it all. Say to yourself, 'Assuming that I *don't* grow out of it, how am I going to deal with adolescence? Who am I, anyway, as of right now? I'm *somebody*, right? And even if I don't change at all, how much will that matter to me? And how much should it matter? And besides, I know I *will* change, sooner or later."

Looking back on her own adolescence, Sue Ashton remembers it as a voyage that had its storms and its pains, but one that was "not especially stormy, not especially painful."

"I'm glad it's over," she said. "I would not do it again, not at all. But I don't think that if I could do it again I'd do things differently."

She thought a moment and then corrected her last statement. "Obviously, I would have done some things differently," she said. "But most things I just wouldn't have any control over. So much of adolescence is just sort of inevitable, and luck. How fast you develop, and when you develop, is just chance. And choice doesn't have that much of a role to play. It helps if you have a sense of humor about the whole thing. You know that you've got to accept it, and you know that you might as well laugh at it, no matter how painful it's going to be, however bitter the laughter might be."

7

Getting Help

The strange, exciting, confusing, and universal process of adolescence is a very big deal. It marks the human being's conversion from childhood to adulthood, the most dramatic change that most of us are likely to experience in our entire lives. It would be strange indeed if we were able to go through such a transformation without experiencing some problems, anxieties, worries, and miscellaneous other hang-ups.

It wouldn't be adolescence without worries about development that's not moving quickly enough (or that has moved too quickly); about your feelings toward your parents and other adults and your classmates; about acne, the opposite sex, sex in general, and life in particular.

We live in a time when people advertise — and we tend to expect — quick cures for practically everything that bothers us. So we might assume there's some instant solution for the problems of adolescence. A cassette tape that walks you through menarche, perhaps, or a one-hour seminar that straightens out all your problems with your parents.

It isn't that way, of course, and it never will be. Adolescence means the pains as well as the joys. Another way of putting it: One of the big values of adolescence (maybe the biggest value of them all) comes in the series of lessons we teach ourselves while we cope with the problems that adolescence presents. Perhaps more than anything else, adolescence is a *learning* experience.

Suppose you wake up one morning and realize that a comment that your father made last night at the dinner table — perhaps it was something about politics, or religion, or the sort of music that you think is terrific but that he thinks is idiotic — is absolutely wrong.

As a tiny child, you learned to *trust* your parents; you learned that they were the source of all wisdom in your life. Above all, you learned that they were *right* about everything.

Now you're older, and you're accumulating evidence that there may be a few gaps in your parents' wisdom — or, worse, that they might be flat-out, downright, 100 percent *wrong* about something. Now, that may create a conflict in your mind. You might find yourself feeling sad, or confused, or angry at the notion that you're rejecting the wisdom of these people who brought you into the world and kept you alive and healthy in it.

An instant cure for that sort of confusion not only wouldn't be helpful; it also would be harmful, because part of your growing-up process — the intensive training course you're taking to become an adult — requires that you figure out how to handle problems, such as the one about your parents' beliefs. You have to struggle with the confusion, frustration, self-doubt, and anger, to work out for yourself the balance between you and your parents, between your wisdom and theirs. You have to learn that there are going to be times when your truth and your parents' truth are in conflict, and you have to learn that it's perfectly possible, and even likely, for such a situation to exist — that you can disagree with your parents without abandoning them. You have to break your connections with childhood, but that doesn't mean you will burn all the bridges between you and your parents. You just build new ones that serve you and them well once you've become an adult like them.

The situation is similar for someone who sees himself as a late bloomer. Suppose it is very obvious to you that you're not only developing physically much more slowly than your classmates, but also that you're never going to be as splendidly developed as some of the people around you. You'll never be the captain of the football team, nor will you ever be the head cheerleader.

You may dream, from time to time, about a secret potion that would transform you overnight into a muscular hunk or a dynamic dish, but the hard truth is that no such potion exists. So what do you do? You learn to live with your body the way it is. More important, you learn to live *within* it. You learn to make the best of what you've got. You use your brain, for one thing. It's the most valuable organ your body has. (It might tell you, without too much heavy thought, that neither football captain nor head cheerleader is among society's more lasting occupations.) If it's excellence and admiration you want, there are a million ways to excel that don't require great physical strength or beauty. If you doubt this, just look at what's been accomplished by people who are *really* physically handicapped. Some of our finest musicians have been blind; one of our presidents was partially paralyzed; a young man ran all the way across Canada to raise money for cancer research, and he had only one leg.

If you don't look like Brooke Shields, then try looking like yourself. Some of Rebecca Wolff's friends think she looks better as Rebecca Wolff than as *any* teen-aged model.

❊   ❊   ❊

There *are* some problems that can occur in adolescence, though, that go beyond the basic, everyday emotional aches and pains of growing up. When they happen, they are bad news, because the young person who seeks help may be told, "Don't worry; you'll grow out of it." In many cases, that advice is correct; but in some, it could only make the problem worse.

Suppose you really *aren't* developing properly. Suppose you're several years into your teens, all your classmates are well on their way to development, and you're still spinning your wheels in childhood. The spurt in growth that marks the beginning of puberty hasn't happened.

You could chew your nails and weep a lot. Or you could seek help in the adult world, which in this case means parents. They can schedule a visit to a physician, perhaps one who specializes in growth difficulties, and the doctor can perform tests that may provide clues as to what's happening. He or she may be able to provide treatment to get your hormonal clockwork back on schedule, or he may assure you that you're well within the developmental range, in which case you can go back to biting your nails for a while longer.

The important thing here is to not let the problem take over your mind and run your life. Help *is* available. It may be embarrassing to go to an adult — your parents, or a physician, or a psychologist or psychiatrist

— and explain your fears about inadequate development. But in the long run, it's the best way.

Concerns about physical development are not the only potentially serious problems of adolescence. Another area in which young people may need help — and it is one that appears to be getting larger all the time — has to do with illegal drugs.

You will encounter some people who argue that the best way to deal with drugs is to never touch them — to live your life as if these substances simply never existed. For some, that might work very nicely. But others might think it's a bit unrealistic; all the evidence shows that drugs are widely available to young people and that many young people take them. It would be foolish not to assume that someone entering puberty will be curious about the drugs that the older kids at school are talking about, just as he's going to be curious about other popular topics of conversation, such as sex, cars, and basketball.

One young person who recently completed adolescence, who was interviewed on the subject of drug use, says it just doesn't make sense for young people or adults to pretend that if we don't talk about drugs, they won't present a problem.

"Drugs are everywhere at this point," said this young woman. "In school, after school, everywhere." This teen-ager is from a big city, where for a long time drugs have been known to be easily available to everyone, be they adult or child. But her friends from suburban communities tell her drugs can be bought there just as easily.

For this young woman, drugs became so much a part of her life that, toward the end of her adolescence, she became seriously harmed by them. After taking a particularly dangerous mixture of drugs she fell into a coma. She survived, but only after spending a good deal of time in medical care.

This person thinks, as do a lot of others who have studied the situation, that young people are drawn more to drugs now because of pressures on their lives that didn't exist in previous generations. "Life is a lot more complicated," she said. "I think that most teen-age suicides probably have to do with drugs in one way or another. Even if there's not a direct connection, I think probably most people who take their lives are involved in drugs because drugs influence your think-ing in ways that can be negative."

This teen-ager said she learned one important thing through her experience with drugs. It's okay to say "No, thank you, I don't want to do it." People who say this needn't worry about being ridiculed, she said; those who take drugs usually respect the choice of someone who declines. If they don't respect it, then maybe you shouldn't respect *them.*

"I've got an interesting situation coming up soon,"

she said, "because all my friends still do drugs, and we're all going to be together this summer. So I'm going to be saying, 'Sorry, it's not for me.' And they're going to have to accept that about me. It's ridiculous to think that they wouldn't accept it, because they *actually are* my friends. And friends stick by you."

In the case of the young woman who faced up to some of the problems that come with using drugs, help came both from the outside world and from within herself: The outside world, which included her parents and medical experts, intervened when she had to have emergency treatment for the coma. And the help from within came when she put her brain to work and calculated the plusses and minuses of doing drugs. She used the mental processes, the new set of standards, that her voyage through adolescence had equipped her with.

There's a great variety of places you can go and things you can do if you need help in your journey toward adulthood. And *everybody* needs help, of one sort or another. Nobody goes through adolescence alone; it would be a dreary voyage indeed if we did.

The biggest single source of help in adolescence (and most other stages of life) comes from talking it over with someone else. The "someone else" doesn't even have to be an expert on the subject, although it would be wise to seek out an expert if your problem is a serious one. For the day-to-day distresses of growing up, though, and even the year-to-year ones, the best prescription is talking it over.

But with whom? Mothers and fathers are one obvious place you might go for advice (parents never run out of that) and commiseration, which is the process of extending sympathy. But although your mother and father are right there (or one of them is, since there are more single-parent families in America now than ever before), and they are ready to help you, and they love you, and they would do anything in the world for you, they may not be the world's best people to talk with. Your adolescence concerns their feelings as well as yours; part of the process you're going through involves breaking and then remaking the connections between parent and child, and a lot of the things you need commiseration with have to do with your feelings toward your parents. Maybe other people would be better sources of help.

For problems that are clearly serious ones, you should seek out expert, professional help from a doctor, a counselor at school, a religious leader. But for the ordinary aches and pains of adolescence, there's another excellent source nearby. It's free of charge, and it's available all day, any day, including weekends and holidays, from someone you already know: your best friends.

Your friends — your "support group," some people

might call them; others refer to them as "peer groups" — may not be any more expert at solving the problems of adolescence than you are, but they're valuable nonetheless. Sue Ashton says, "They may not be too constructive when you go to them with a problem. They may just say, 'Yeah, well, don't worry about it.' But that's where people go first — to their friends."

These friends offer a kind of help that nobody else can supply: proof that you're not alone. It's very helpful to know that you're not the only girl in your class who's waging what appears to be a losing war against pimples, or that you're not the only boy who wonders when his voice is going to change. Friends can be vital sources of information about the opposite sex. (A lot of the information may not be correct, but at least it's better than no information at all, and it shows you that you're not the only one who's curious.)

These support groups can be found practically anywhere, but it stands to reason that most of them are made up of your friends at school. As Sue Ashton observed, however, a lot of information can come from just being a member of a large family.

People who have studied adolescence have found that the peer group is a valuable part of the adolescent's voyage. Such groups can be harmful, as when they gang up against a kid who's too short, or too ugly, or too awkward, and make life miserable for him. But they also serve as a sort of culture that the adolescent can live in while he's going through the process. The Committee on Adolescence, in its report, wrote that "The peer group, greatly expanded by modern means of transportation and communication, today constitutes an adolescent 'culture' which has its own language, modes and methods of solving problems, and philosophies."

Irene Josselyn, the psychiatrist who wrote *The Adolescent and His World*, points out that the peer group is a powerful force for conformity. It "supplies the answer to almost any question," she wrote, "whether it involves wearing a hat to town, straightening bobby socks so they are neater, wearing blue jeans that still retain their original color, being sexually promiscuous, or cheating in examinations." Most importantly, the group serves for its members "as a relative island of security in a tumultuous world. It has protected the individual from becoming lost in the tortuous paths and possibly the blind alleys of the psychological maze of adolescence."

Membership in a peer group is not for life. People can move from group to group pretty easily, just as they will do as adults in their social lives later. In fact, the adolescent's peer group–support group is in many ways a younger model of the society she's going to be functioning in a little later on. The skills you learn in

81

your dealings with friends now will form the basis of the way you deal with people later. Everything in adolescence is learning.

When you get through puberty's gate, you're covered with confusion. You overdo everything. You have the feeling that the world is treating you unfairly (and part of the time you're right). You love your parents, and you know they love you, but your dealings with them have been described with such terms as "rebellion" and "revolt."

You're awkward, but sometimes you're graceful. Your body is all out of proportion, but sometimes it's beautiful. You realize, in the midst of all this, that the bodies of other people are beautiful. You're attracted to them, and if they have beautiful minds as well, you're in heaven. You're having fun, but you're also mired in misery. You're both "bewildered" and "bewildering." You're stuck in a space warp between the time when you only receive nurture and the time when you give nurture. You, in collaboration with someone else, can produce a child, a living human being; but society doesn't want you to right now and will probably punish you if you do. A lot of what you hear, about everything from sex to automobile ownership, is "wait a few more years. . . ." But you're living very much in the present, and "a few more years" seems like a century.

You, your ideas, your loyalty, and especially your money are eagerly sought by the media and the other representatives of society who want to sell you things, from the people who write television commercials to the executives of tennis shoe factories to promoters from phonograph record companies. In turn, these people want to sell *you* — or at least what they fantasize is your style of life, your enthusiasm for living, your tastes in clothes and music and even haircuts — to the older members of society who have been told by the media that they must "stay young" at any cost. Talk about confusion!

You may be enraged by the belief that you've got a fully mature brain that just happens to be stuck inside a not-quite-yet mature body and that people should take you a lot more seriously than they do. And yet you may suspect the real truth: Your brain isn't quite mature yet, either. It's waiting for the stuff brains like most to chew on: experience.

You're gathering that experience right now. And you're using that experience — the ways you react to the everyday things that happen around you, the ways in which you deal with other people — to build the structure that will soon become the adult you. You're writing your code of ethics, your set of standards, the rules that are going to determine how you deal with the rest of the world for the rest of your life.

A few years ago, your parents created a person and

brought it into the world. Now you're putting the finishing touches on the job. It's pretty exciting, when you think about it — particularly when you remember that what you're learning now is going to be the raw material for one of the biggest construction projects in the history of our planet. You're going to change the world, literally, with your thinking. Every generation does it, and every generation gets a chance to do it right.

Index

Accidents, 11
Acne, 27, 52
Adolescence and adolescents
  and anger, 13, 73
  and apprehension, 31, 45,
    71–84
  awkwardness, 21, 22, 82
  definitions and descrip-
    tions, 10–18, 61–70, 72,
    82
  discovery of one's sexual
    maturity, 42
  emotional changes, 30–43,
    45–51
  and idealism, 14
  impulsive behavior and
    excess, 13, 14, 15, 41
  as learning experience,
    72–73, 81–82, 83–84
  and loneliness, 56
  and love of fun, 15
  and media, 51–53, 83
  and nutrition, 28

  physical changes, 19–29,
    45–51
  and school, 5
  and sense of humor, 70
  stages and duration, 3, 7,
    17, 19–29
  standards, 3, 24, 40
  as universal experience, 7,
    16, 17, 58, 67
  "vacations" from tension,
    35, 63–64
  as a "voyage," 12
  see also Support and "sup-
    port groups"; Drugs
Adulthood, 31, 40
  freedoms and obligations, 31
  lack of standards for, 40
  see also Rites of passage
Adults, and adolescence, 1,
    13, 15, 16, 32, 36, 38–41,
    42, 53, 54, 56, 60, 75–76
  see also Parents; School;
    Society

85

Index

Index